BALANCE SHEETS & BREAKTHROUGHS

A YOUNG FEMALE'S ACCOUNTING JOURNEY

SHAKIRA JOHNSON

Balance Sheets & Breakthroughs

Book design by Pen2publishing

Copyright © 2024

All rights reserved. This book is protected by the copyright laws of the United States of America. This book may not be reprinted or copied for commercial use or profit. The use of short passages or page copying for personal use or group study is permitted and encouraged.

Table of Contents

Acknowledgements v

Foreword vii

Chapter 1 – Introduction 1

Chapter 2 - Early inspiration 3

Chapter 3 – Embracing the challenges of the first job 7

Chapter 4 – Navigating early career challenges. 11

Chapter 5 – Building a strong foundation 15

Chapter 6 – Professional growth 20

Chapter 7 – Navigating the workplace 26

Chapter 8 – Embracing leadership opportunities 34

Chapter 9 – Achieving work-life integration 40

Chapter 10 – Looking to the future 47

Chapter 11 – Achieving success 53

Chapter 12 – Conclusion 57

ACKNOWLEDGEMENTS

First, I give thanks to God who presented me with the opportunity and the ability to write and release this book. I never pictured myself as a writer but through each chapter, I was able to express myself with the help of God. This book comes on the heels of one of the most emotional experiences and setbacks that I have had in life, and whilst I wanted many times to give up, God gave me purpose and placed people around me to pull a vision out of me and help bring it to life. This book would not be a reality today without God being my strength.

To my friend and mentor Dr. George Greaves, I am indeed thankful for your unwavering support, and encouragement throughout this journey. You believed in me even when I didn't believe in myself. I thank you for all your guidance along the way and celebrations of all the wins no matter how small. You have definitely been the light in a dark place for me. You have poured into me in immeasurable ways and pushed me to see myself through an untainted lens. I truly appreciate you.

To my support system, "3 Johnsons and a Springer"; Dominic, Shavonne, Felicia and Roxanne, this is the true definition of family. Each of you have been a sounding board on this project. You always have my back and did well at keeping this project a secret until I was ready for the world to know.

To my mum and dad, Denise and Douglas, I hope I have made you proud. Thank you for setting the foundation for me to pursue education and to do my best at whatever I put my hands to.

I also want to acknowledge my wonderful friend Janee, the true definition of a ride or die. Your excitement since I shared the idea has been infectious. It has helped me to keep this project in mind. Thank you for being my biggest cheerleader over the years.

I extend a heartfelt thank you to everyone who has positively impacted my professional journey. I have made it this far because of you.

Lastly, to all my readers, thank you for trusting me enough to grab a copy of this book. I trust that it will be worth the read.

FOREWORD

It is rare to encounter a voice as powerful, authentic, and transformative as Shakira Johnson's. From the moment I met her and heard her story, I knew that her words would resonate deeply, not just because of her remarkable journey, but because of her unwavering dedication to sharing it with courage and clarity. Her story is remarkable and must be heard by her selected audience.

In today's world, where many are searching for meaning and connection, Shakira's work offers a beacon of hope. Her ability to navigate the complexities of life, embrace its challenges, and rise above adversity is not only inspiring but instructive. Her experiences, shaped by grit, determination, and a resilient spirit, have given her unique insights into the human condition—insights that she now graciously shares with us in this book.

I am fortunate to know her as a friend. The quality and depth of her story has given me hope that excellence is still a quality to be achieved. This powerful story speaks of a divine connection, a powerful professional journey and a reality of finding how to change adversity into remarkable success. She is a woman of graceful passion and convincing determination.

What sets Shakira apart is her openness and the palpable sincerity in every word she writes. She doesn't sugarcoat the difficult parts of her journey, nor does she shy away from hard truths. Instead, she embraces them, allowing us to see both the struggles and the victories in equal measure. Her words serve as a reminder that we are not alone in our battles, and that even in our darkest moments, there is a path forward.

This book is more than just a reflection of Shakira's personal growth; it is a guide for anyone seeking to navigate life's challenges with grace, purpose, and resilience. Each page invites the reader to reflect, to heal, and to grow. Whether you're facing your own struggles, seeking inspiration, or simply wanting to learn from someone who has walked through the fire and emerged stronger, this book will speak to you.

As you embark on this journey with Shakira, prepare yourself to be moved, to be challenged, and ultimately, to be empowered. This is more than a book—it's a call to action, an invitation to live more fully, more authentically, and with a deeper understanding of our own personal and professional potential.

It is with great honor and admiration that I introduce you to Shakira Johnson's incredible work. May her story inspire you as it has inspired and impacted me.

George N Greaves Eds. ED (ABD)

CHAPTER 1

INTRODUCTION

Every young person imagines one thing in life: success. Different individuals may have varying perspectives on how success looks or is defined, but ultimately, we all desire to excel at something We want to be recognized by others positively, in an outstanding way. Some aspire to be great athletes, models, clothing designers, engineers, or doctors. For some females, being a housewife or stay at home mom, is what they envision as success. Being able to travel the world without financial limitations may be the goal post for others. Some may be environmentally focused and want to contribute to the quest of reducing our carbon footprint. Others just want to make their parents proud. Then there is the rare handful, the ones who don't know any better; the ones who define success as being an accomplished accountant.

I always knew I wanted to be successful in life, but to say that I knew I wanted to be a Finance professional would be a far stretch from the truth. The reality is, being born and raised on a little island in the Caribbean, success was defined for us in my era as being a doctor, lawyer, or accountant. Our schools' curricula were heavily influenced by the British system and in some ways very limited. The courses offered at the secondary school level generally pushed you in one of the directions mentioned above if you were academically inclined. The truth is, I stumbled into accounting, I had no sense of what I was doing, what it entailed, or where it would take me, but one thing is for sure, it has been a journey.

Realistically, most things in life don't come easy and regardless of the path we choose, career or otherwise, challenges will present themselves. Ultimately, success is dependent on one's mindset, resilience, and ability to adapt to changes, situations, and circumstances as they come along, most often unpredictably. The journey will not be a straight line. There will be moments which may require you to stop, pivot and even turn around completely. The key is to keep going and not give up.

My career path started as an auditor. I followed this path for just over ten years, after which I transitioned to a Finance role within the Banking industry for four years and finally to where I am now. Some fifteen years later, I am no longer that uncertain university student or timid auditor. Instead, I hold the position of Assistant Vice President of Finance at the largest insurance company within the Caribbean region. Did I imagine that this is where I would be at this point in my life? I most certainly did not foresee it. However, having reached this far in my career, the purpose of this book is to guide young aspiring professionals on how they too can excel in the field of accountancy or even beyond using examples from my journey. Each of us will have a unique journey along the way, but quite often there may be an overlap of experiences at some point. My aim is to help you to navigate some of these experiences, even better than I did mine. I hope that this book is insightful and provides key strategies and tips that can be applied to your individual career journeys and lead you on a path of success.

CHAPTER 2

EARLY INSPIRATION

Growing up I had a love for Mathematics. I was a good Mathematics student. My friend in secondary school at the time suggested that I should try Accounts because it was all about numbers. That was how my journey began. I studied Accounts at the secondary school level, did well in the subject and progressed to 6th Form. There were several teachers along the way who saw my potential and encouraged me tremendously. Whilst my love for Mathematics was still present and I wished to pursue it further, for some reason, Accounting came more naturally. Pursuing Mathematics soon became a lost thought and even my grades began to highlight that I was good at Accounts. It therefore made sense, and with the prompting of some teachers that the natural progression was to pursue a Bachelor of Science Degree in Accounting and Economics at the university level (University of the West Indies). Throughout the 3-year program at university, I came to realize that I had little interest in Economics, whilst my fascination with Accounting grew. To be honest, I applied for a double major in Accounting and Economics simply because one of my 6th Form teachers indicated that it would make me more marketable upon the completion of university. In all fairness, it made my university life a little harder. However, what I always advise people who are studying is that once you have that degree, no one can take it away from you. Despite never entering an economic field on completion of university, I can still proudly say that I also have a degree in Economics.

I never really had a clear career path. In some ways I was just moving with the tides of life. Letting life happen or going with the flow as we often say. Some may frown on my confession of not having a plan, but life has a way of sometimes placing you where you need to be at the right time. Don't get me wrong, having a plan is not a bad thing. It helps keep you focused and can be a roadmap for your journey. Coming to the end of my three-year degree program, I had given little thought to what would come next i.e., no plan. If I could take a minute to drop a snippet of advice here, it would be:

Develop a Plan

The plan doesn't need to be super detailed. Take some time to think about where you would like to end up. Have a goal, a practical one and begin to look for opportunities to position yourself towards achieving that goal.

In my country, it was frequent practice of representatives of the Big Four audit firms to have workshops for final year accounting students. It was somewhat of a scouting exercise for these companies, where they came and spoke to students about their respective organizations or did mock interviews to identify potential employees. It was at one of those workshops that I decided that auditing is where I would attempt to start my career. Of course I didn't know what I was getting into, but I will talk about that in more detail later.

Create A Strong Résumé

I was fortunate to have access to a service offered by the university which helped students to create appropriate résumés. With the technology available at our fingertips today, you don't necessarily need to sit across the room from someone to carve out a résumé. There are numerous templates and examples that you can draw references from. However, it would still be advisable to have someone who is already in a professional environment to give it a glance over.

After two rounds of interviews, I began my professional career as an auditor at one of the Big Four audit firms. I remember stepping into the first interview feeling nervous and uncertain. To be honest I had no real idea of what the role that I was applying for entailed. Nor was I smart enough to have those type of questions lined up to ask in the interview to obtain more insight. I just knew that everyone was buzzing about getting one of these jobs and I wanted to secure my spot. I left the interview feeling more nervous than when I arrived. "Did I do a good job? Did I wow them? Maybe I could have answered that question better." All of these were the thoughts racing through my mind at the end of the interview. These feelings of doubt and uncertainty after an interview are not uncommon, however, the more you prepare for the interview, the less weight you feel after giving it your all. Spend time researching potential interview questions and carve out your responses. Have trial runs with your friends or family members to become more comfortable and confident in speaking. Amidst all the nervousness and self-doubt, apparently, I did a good enough job to get hired.

In many ways, getting this far in the journey was due to taking that little suggestion from a friend. Often in life, we end up on paths that others envision for us. Some people may see potential in us that we don't see in ourselves. A little guidance sometimes is good. I believe if that childhood friend knew the extent of my success today, she would not attribute any of it to her words to me so many years ago. In this instance that suggested path worked well towards me being where I am now.

CHAPTER 3

EMBRACING THE CHALLENGES OF THE FIRST JOB

The transition from the world of studying to the world of work is not particularly an easy one. Some of us are good at adapting to change whilst others struggle with the concept of something new. This was no longer studying at your own pace, procrastinating when you want and catching up after. This was now the real world. You no longer operate on your time, but you now report to a boss and form a part of a team which needs to operate as a well-oiled machine. Many of us hated group projects at school and even more so at university, now the world of work encourages collaboration and teamwork at a level never experienced before. However, unlike university, you have no choice but to play along. This transition from academia to the professional world will take some time and adjustment.

My biggest challenge entering the workplace was that of a major knowledge gap. We often like to think that once we have the university degree or qualification, we have what it takes to get the job done. We think we know it all. We have all the theory down pack. In reality, there is a major disparity between understanding the theory and knowing how to apply it in the real world. Does this mean that you are dumb? Absolutely not. It simply means that there is a learning curve that you must overcome before becoming this expert that you think you already are simply because of a certificate. I don't mean to be harsh, but this is often the reality in most professions. Yes, you worked hard to attain that certificate, but without the practical application, it is nothing more than a piece of paper. You are now starting at ground zero again. The playing field is levelled, and this is the starting point of your real learning journey. There is much growth and development to come, and you must be prepared to embrace it.

You Do Not Know It All

Be open to learning new things and unlearning some of the textbook applications. The latter may sound strange, but one must be agile and able to adapt quickly. What might be the perfect application from a textbook perspective sometimes doesn't apply to the situations that we face in the work environment, so being teachable is important. No one likes the newcomer who acts like they know it all. This attitude exudes arrogance and that definitely will not help you to progress in your career.

Three weeks of training and my brain was fried, scrambled even. There were new concepts to learn, along with much technical jargon and software that I was never exposed to before. Those three weeks were grueling. After a while, there was little room in my brain to absorb all the information being thrown at me. I felt lost, confused, but what I realized was that I wasn't alone. Within that period of training, friendships started to develop, people were comfortable sharing, and it was then that some of my colleagues confessed that it too was a bit much for them. Oh, the sigh of relief I let out, knowing that I wasn't a complete dunce. Others just were not getting it either. There then was the expectation that you retained what was taught in those three weeks and would be able to apply it once placed on an assignment. Just in case you didn't know, audit is no joke. Basically, I went from one classroom: university, to another classroom: audit training and then into the field. It was tough. This experience was the beginning of my first lesson in giving myself grace.

Aside from bridging knowledge gaps, another challenge is adapting to culture. I once heard someone say that culture is the strongest force in any organization. It shapes and models how people operate and interact in the workplace. People often fail in new environments because they don't understand the culture. Take time out to understand the culture, the mode of operation. Be observant, understand the chain of command. Most importantly, if unsure, ask questions. This is where mentorship comes into play. Sheryl Sandberg said "Mentorship is crucial for professional growth and personal development. It provides guidance, support, and an invaluable sounding board."

Seek Out Good Mentors

The first organization I worked for already had a mentorship program in place. All new hires were assigned to a mentor. This was someone who provided guidance, helped you carve out your performance goals and objectives for each year and then created a plan for you to reach those goals within the specified time frame. Every organization might not have a formal mentorship program, however that should not be a deterrent. Seek out those who according to Michelle Obama "encourages growth and provides a positive example to follow." Each organization will have a mixed bag of people. Some who are just there to collect a pay cheque, some whose focus is on their personal growth and development and others who wish to help others excel. Seek out the latter and watch your career transform. My mentor was assigned to me. I didn't get to choose who I wanted, but I would say he was a good fit. A man who operated on integrity and principles and was keen to see me reach my full potential. We went on separate paths years later but to this day, we still stay connected and I still very much value his advice. A good mentor will bring out the best in you and help you navigate the challenges associated with career progression.

CHAPTER 4

NAVIGATING EARLY CAREER CHALLENGES

Various challenges are likely to arise early in one's career. I spoke earlier about the knowledge gap and adapting to culture. These are just a few of the more common challenges. However, the number of challenges lined up waiting for you just to bump into them are endless. I remember one of the first questions my mentor asked me was how far I was willing to go in the organization. Being the naive overachiever that I am, my quick response was that I wanted to be a Partner of the firm. In hindsight I often laugh at the thought of myself as a Partner. Looking around I quickly observed that the firm was primarily staffed by females, yet the male to female ratio of Partners was heavily weighted towards the males. It was at this point that I noticed that whilst females are often the hardest workers, the roles of leadership were still very much male dominated. The tides have shifted over the period during which I have been in this profession, and I have seen more females taking on leadership roles. This is a positive movement for those of you now entering the profession, but for the old schoolers like me, it meant that we had very few female role models to look up to. Females were not considered leaders. Society was still in an age of patriarchy where the men were the leaders, and the women were the support system. Along with my age working against me so was my gender.

 I recall an experience going to an audit client, arranging a meeting with a junior employee of the client to discuss several items. About 10 minutes into the meeting her boss walked by, looked upset, called her a few minutes later and she expressed that she could no longer continue the meeting because she had other work to do. I made no progress on that day. When my manager asked me for a status update at the end of the day, I had to explain that my meeting with the client was cut short and the list of outstanding items remained unchanged from the previous day. Knowing that we were hard pressed with deadlines, my manager set up a meeting with her, myself, and the employee's boss, to understand why we couldn't get time with his employee to discuss matters. This is where it got nasty. This is where I realized that I was not respected because of my age and gender. The individual proceeded to indicate that I spent most of the day with his staff member (now remember I said I met with her for about 10 mins before he interrupted the meeting). He blatantly said that I was incompetent if after spending a full day with his staff, I was able to achieve nothing and told my manager very matter-of-factly, that if I can't get the job done, they should find someone else who can. I was infuriated. The audacity of this man to sit there and tell lies and use those lies to insult me. I was ready to cuss him out, but obviously that wouldn't be the professional approach. I opened my mouth to defend myself and my manager placed her hand on my leg as a signal to say let her handle it.

I left his office that day feeling immensely angry and the frustration of not being able to call him out on his lies was more than I could bear. My manager and I took the elevator back down without saying a word to each other. I felt humiliated. I made it back to the audit room, placed my laptop on the desk and I went to the bathroom and cried. Not out of sadness but sheer anger that I had no choice but to keep locked on the inside.

Never Let Them See You Cry

It is okay to cry but do it in private, pull yourself back together and put back on your game face before facing the world again. You see, crying is seen as a sign of weakness, especially in females. We are seen as too sensitive and too emotional. Once they see you cry, they will never take you seriously as a professional. I have had many days of tears and many days of frustration. I will admit that despite this advice that I am giving to you, I did have moments where I broke down in tears in front of others. I won't fool you into thinking that I always managed to keep it together. However, after those tears fell, I always walked out, whether from an office, a bathroom or from my car with my head held high. My spirit might have been bruised but I surely wasn't defeated.

Fast forward to the next day when the Partner at my firm got a wind of the situation and confronted the individual. Needless to say, that man never said a word to me again. I would always greet him politely in passing with a "Good Morning" or "Good Afternoon" to which his only response would be a grunt. I found it absolutely hilarious. I bet that he almost caught a heart attack when 15 years later

I was introduced within his organization as Assistant Vice President of Finance, but I am getting ahead of myself a bit.

A career in audit is driven by deadlines, as the first part of the word eludes, you almost feel as though you will die trying to finish an audit on time, especially those that are governed by regulatory guidelines and come under heavy scrutiny. This brings about another challenge which starts early in your career and has a way of following you along the journey unless you intentionally put measures in place to avoid it. I am talking about those favorite buzzwords that are thrown around ever so often: work life balance.

Find and Create the Balance You Need

A career in accountancy can take over your entire life if you allow it. It is common to look around and see some of your friends who chose different career paths enjoying their lives whilst you feel like you are always stuck behind the computer with a looming deadline. It is at this point that people often feel like quitting and starting over. Here is my advice; your boss will not know the things which are of value to you. His/her focus is on delivering output, meeting expectations etc. The onus is really on you to identify what you need to maintain a good mental balance. If spending time with family is important to you, carve out days for family. If going for walks is calming, take an hour after work to do some walking, even if it means logging back on afterwards to complete the task that you were working on. If you love going to the gym, maybe going on evenings might not be feasible, try going on mornings instead. Find a rhythm that works for you.

CHAPTER 5

BUILDING A STRONG FOUNDATION

Building a strong foundation is two-fold. It involves continuous education and certification and building a support network. Journey with me as we examine both in detail.

To progress in the field of accountancy, having a university degree is not enough. These degrees teach you the basics but to truly advance, further education is required such as an accounting designation. Acquiring a designation positions you well for future career development. It is key to career advancement and makes you more marketable in the industry. If you look at advertisements for senior accounting positions, they typically ask that the candidate has an accounting designation. The choice of designation is mostly linked to your location or where you plan to work eventually.

Some of the more recognized designations are listed below.

1. *Association of Chartered Certified Accountants (ACCA):* This is a globally recognized UK based

organization which focuses on financial management, taxation, audit, and financial reporting.
2. **Certified Public Accountant (CPA):** This is recognized primarily in the United States with a focus on auditing, taxation, financial accounting, and business law.
3. **Chartered Accountant (CA):** Mostly Canadian based with an emphasis on financial accounting, audit, taxation, and management accounting.
4. **Certified Management Accountant (CMA):** This is recognized globally, particularly in the United States. Its focus is on management accounting, financial management, and strategic management.

Do your research. See which program best suits you and I would suggest getting started within six months to a year of your first job. What I have found is that persons who delay starting beyond that suggested period, seldom start at all or find it more difficult to complete after delaying for a few years. Do it while you are still youthful, while your brain is still accustomed to the concept of studying. Working and studying is always a challenge especially in a fast-paced working environment. Consideration must be given to the way in which you learn best. I personally learn better in a classroom setting. When I pursued my ACCA designation, classes were being offered in a physical classroom on weekends. For me, the direct interaction with the lecturer and students in the same room enhanced my learning experience. Where I struggled, was working late hours during the week, and then having to head to class early on Saturdays and Sundays. Additionally, finding the time to study and practice questions outside of the classroom was difficult. Burn out was a real thing. However, if you really want something you have to go after it purposefully. Now, particularly since COVID, online classes have increased in popularity and offerings, and some find it more convenient than a classroom setting. Again, I say, determine what type of learning works best for you and give it your all.

What is not to be taken lightly are the demands of these designations. They are not a walk in the park. Don't be discouraged or demotivated if the grades are not what you are accustomed to or even if you fail some of the courses. I thought I was a top student at university until I met ACCA. Pursuing this designation humbled me. The grades that once came with ease, I now had to work extremely hard to come close to. I did two examinations per sitting. In the classroom, I thought I had it covered. Doing the practice questions, I was certain that I understood the concepts. However, when I came face to face with those examination papers it was a whole different story. My first two exams, my grades were in the fifties. It was unbelievable. Truthfully, whilst they were still considered passes, I was ashamed of those grades. I was a ninety percent and above type of student. Grades in the fifties just weren't my thing. They shattered my confidence. This was another point in life where I asked myself what have I gotten into? I had to try harder, I had to put in more effort and most importantly I had to identify the areas of weakness which were causing me to score low. My low grades weren't because I didn't understand. In most cases it was time management that worked against me in the exams. It is as if the exams are preparing you for the deadline driven work environments. Knowing what to do is not enough, if you don't manage your time accordingly to actually get it done. If you are serious about pursuing a designation, you must be fully committed to it and be prepared to make sacrifices. I assure you, that those sacrifices will yield rewards at the end. I completed my designation in just over 3 years failing one exam along the way, but I never gave up.

Building a support network is critical. I referred to the importance of finding good mentors in the field earlier, but building a professional network is equally as important. Accounting is one profession that spans across a broad cross section of industries. If you think about it, every well-established business needs at least an accountant or on a bigger scale a fully complemented Finance Department as part of its operations. Persons working in Finance across different industries, will become experts in certain areas along the way. Networking is therefore key. It allows you to build relationships, a circle who you can bounce concepts off of.

At the beginning of my career, I was very timid. If I walked into a room with strangers, I would stay in a corner and not interact. Let me tell you now, that approach will hinder your growth. I had to adapt, and now I am very much comfortable speaking to strangers. This shift was needed to effectively network.

Make Connections: They Will Serve You Well

You can build your network internally, i.e. within the organization where you are employed or externally. From an external perspective, most countries have professional associations for accountants. Register, attend conferences, seminars etc. which provides a great learning ground. Even attend the social functions arranged by the professional associations. Volunteer to be members of committees in your industry or even with the professional association for accountants.

Social media can also be a strategy for networking if used correctly. Professional sites such as LinkedIn bring professionals and industry leaders together. In this space you can engage in discussions on trending topics, share your views and listen to the perspective of others.

The greatest benefit from having a good support network is being able to leverage knowledge. To this day, I have maintained contact with persons from every organization where I have been employed. I have been able to reach out to them at times for guidance on a particular subject matter. It is impossible to know it all, but if each person in the network has some distinct knowledge, it gives you access to that knowledge and vice versa. Having that network support system also opens doors for opportunities. Think about it, you may have made a good impression with someone whom you networked with, and you might just be the first person they call or recommend when a job opportunity becomes available. Making these meaningful connections will support your personal and professional growth and can elevate your career to heights never imagined.

CHAPTER 6

PROFESSIONAL GROWTH

Those who excel in a career path do so because they refuse to remain stagnant. They seek out opportunities for growth and development. In the natural, we are born as babies, but we do not stay in that state of infancy forever. Naturally we grow, we learn new things, we mature. The same holds true in the professional realm. We ought to grow and develop. Some aspire to grow and are driven by a desire deep inside, whilst for others the growth process just comes with the territory. In my role as auditor, I had that desire to grow, I wanted to be promoted year after year, to at least reach the position of manager. This goal required the development of both technical skills and soft skills.

Quite a bit of emphasis is placed on being technically strong. We like to speak of people being smart and often, the softer skills are overlooked. I always prided myself in my ability to learn something and apply it. If you broke it down for me once properly, I was sure to catch on. I took responsibility for my own learning. If I didn't understand something I either researched it until I got it, or I relied on my network to help me grasp the concept.

Having a questioning mind is one technical skill which is critical in the field of accounting.

Be Curious: It Doesn't Kill the Cat

I had a number of people say to me that I catch on well because I am curious. Curiosity is not as bad a trait as some would like us to believe. I love to understand not just my piece of the puzzle but how it all fits together. That is how my technical know-how grew. Sometimes this curiosity rewarded me with more work, but I saw it as for the greater good. Often when I began to dissect procedures or results and ask why we did this versus that, the usual response was "this is how it was always done." With a little digging in some instances, I was able to unravel that something wasn't being done right and no one noticed because they didn't take time to understand the "why" behind what they were doing. That same approach also allowed me to find inefficiencies and recommend more efficient ways of getting to the same result without compromising the work output. All of the above are examples of being technically strong, seeing the bigger picture.

A competent accountant needs strong analytical skills. This goes beyond, looking at or adding numbers. It goes beyond getting a balance sheet or a cash flow to balance. Instead, being analytical allows the numbers to speak to you whilst you use the numbers to tell a story. Much of the technical skills associated with your professional growth will come from on-the-job experience, training programs and your own desire to seek out further knowledge. The ability to problem solve is also one of the greatest technical assets an accountant can have. Trust me when I say that in accounting, you will stumble across a lot of problems, sometimes more that we care to solve. The key is to be able to look beyond the surface, identify the root cause. This will make a lot of problems easier to solve and less likely to repeat.

Another key skill is being able to effectively manage time. There is always some looming deadline, some last-minute request, or some level of pressure. This skill comes with practice. Many accountants are yet to master it, but it is a skill that will serve you well.

Being technically strong is only half of the journey. It will open some doors but when paired with the soft skills, it will present you with many more opportunities. Having the soft skills are too often undervalued in the accounting profession, but they are not to be left out. The epitome of professional development is to be a good leader, one of integrity. What I wish for you never to forget, is that a good leader is both technically strong and possesses the softer skills.

Take Time to Develop the Soft Skills

What are the softer skills you may ask. I will touch on a few in this chapter.

Putting yourself in the other person's shoes; showing empathy towards others. Everything I do is hinged on the golden rule. That is how I live my life from day to day. "Do unto others as you would have them do unto you." For me that sums up kindness and being understanding. We are all human beings; we have our good days and our bad days. Many persons are dealing with personal issues outside of the workplace that may require a bit of understanding on the leaders' part without allowing employees to become complacent or take empathy for granted. Many times, I have been on the receiving end of leaders who took out their personal problems on me in a professional setting. It wasn't a good feeling, and I vowed never to do the same to those who I would lead. There were days when I pulled up in the car park at work, cried my eyes out because of some personal issue, wiped my tears away, and walked into that building and treated staff respectfully, fairly and gave them the support they needed to succeed. To this day I see it as my duty to others to simply treat them as human beings and not robots behind a computer.

Be an example of integrity for others to follow. I spent my entire career working hard, not because I was trying to take over anyone's job but because I wanted to be the best version of me. I didn't take short cuts; I didn't kiss up to the bosses. I could have said this differently, but I chose to keep it professional. I simply did the best I could every day. I stuck to my word and tried to deliver every time. I have come across a few people in my career who got where they are because they kissed up to the bosses. That approach may put you a few steps ahead of your peers for a while but trust me when I say that it will be temporary. Be honest about your work and who you are. I remember one manager saying to me that I excelled because they took me under their wing. I am not an arrogant person, but that comment offended me because I knew I was putting in the work, day and night and my progress was not linked to them in any way. I refused to let that individual make such a powerful claim over my efforts and success. How did I navigate that? I asked to work on different assignments, completely unrelated and unaffiliated with that individual to prove that my integrity wasn't compromised. I made it evident that I gave my best effort every day and surely the rewards for my efforts came.

If I can lay heavy on one soft skill, it is to be able to communicate effectively. We take the ability to effectively communicate for granted too much. A leader who lacks proper communication skills is a big pet peeve of mine. Like oh my gosh, can you say what you mean, can you take a minute to listen, can you stop interrupting when I am answering the question you asked, can the tone of your emails be less aggressive? These are things that happen in the workplace daily of which we need to be mindful of. The way you interact with people sets the foundation for their responsiveness to asks of them. People are not mind readers so be clear and concise about your expectations of others. This eliminates so many issues up front.

As a young female, one skill I value immensely is the ability to positively influence others, specifically young people. One must be able to provide mentoring and coaching in such a way as to motivate persons. This skill develops over time, as you progress in your career. As you become more confident in who you are, you will begin to feel more comfortable in being a voice of influence and change.

Hone those softer skills with the technical knowhow and watch your career accelerate. One doesn't work well without the other. They are equally important. Many of the junior staff that I have had the opportunity to work with and even my peers often commented on how much they valued me, mostly because of my interactions with them. They valued sharing of knowledge, listening, allowing them to have a voice, acknowledging their suggestions and providing technical guidance. Trust me when I say that effectively combining these two skill sets is the key to success.

Give Yourself Grace

One may wonder how this ties into professional growth, but it plays a crucial role. Sometimes we are too hard on ourselves. We can become so driven that the pressure we put on ourselves to grow or to get it right each time actually becomes detrimental. Giving yourself grace means extending patience, understanding, kindness, and most importantly acceptance towards oneself. It acknowledges our humanity and propensity to make mistakes and dispels the concept of perfection. As you grow professionally, you are likely to make mistakes, you may struggle to understand a specific concept, it may take you some time to become fully integrated into a new team. You must recognize that this is all part of your learning and development. Do not beat yourself up when you have these experiences. Allow yourself the time and space to grow and improve without putting undue pressure on yourself to be perfect. Practise speaking positive words to yourself. Acknowledge and celebrate your wins, no matter how small and reaffirm yourself when you make mistakes that you are still capable. The aim is to create a positive nurturing environment for yourself. Remember that you are deserving of the same kindness and understanding that you extend to others.

CHAPTER 7

NAVIGATING THE WORKPLACE

Throughout my post graduate career, I have worked in three different organizations and the workplace dynamic in each was drastically different. Each environment had its own culture which brought along with it a unique set of issues or challenges.

Today we give fancy names to issues that have been prevalent for some time but were overlooked for many years. Issues such as gender bias, gender equality, diversity, and inclusion. These topics now dominate many workplace conversations and programs which aim to treat everyone fairly and with respect, despite gender, ethnicity, age and more recently sexual orientation and gender association.

Strangely enough in addition to male versus female issues, during my career I also had challenges with other females. I was recently introduced to a concept known as Queen Bee Syndrome. This is described as a situation where a woman in a position of authority or leadership mostly in a male-dominated environment distances herself from other women and may even undermine their advancement. I experienced this first-hand. There were women who I met during my career who I considered as brilliant minds, excellent at what they did, female bosses in their own right. The issue was, they treated other females like crap. In the initial stages they were persons who I wanted to emulate, who I aspired to be like, but my feelings towards them soon changed upon realizing that they had no intention of seeing other women excel. These women who should have been role models for other young females to follow offered very little support or mentorship to females, appeared to perceive other women to be a direct threat or competition and instead of nurturing, their response was to tear down other aspiring females. Just like in the bee world, there can only be one queen among the males; that was their thought process. The effect of it was that other females with plenty potential left these organizations because of the effect of Queen Bee Syndrome. To the females reading this book, don't be a queen bee. Encourage, mentor, show appreciation, and help other aspiring females find their way.

Over the years, I found it easier to work with a male leader than with a female. I will probably get knocked for this comment but based on my experience females sometimes create a hostile environment to work in. How did I overcome this? One simple yet genuine hack.

Kill Them with Kindness (But Don't Suck Up)

People tend to warm up to me quickly because I show genuine interest. I have had instances where coworkers labelled someone as antisocial, and I was able to get that person to open up and interact with me and others differently, simply because I showed kindness every day. Little things like walking past an office and stopping by to say good morning and asking how they were. For many females, children are their soft spot and because I genuinely have a love for children, those types of conversations helped me to connect with others. One may also offer to do little tasks for them e.g. "I am going for stationary. Do you need anything." What may seem like insignificant acts can be the stepping stone for building positive working relationships.

    I distinctly remember being placed on an assignment and everyone on the team warned me about a particular client who by their experiences "hated the auditors", "was difficult to work with" and "was just mean". I never let people push their impression of anyone on me. I feel people out for myself. Every day I walked into that office space, I greeted the lady pleasantly, I wished her a good day and I tried to engage her in a little small talk day by day. I made little remarks like "I will try not to bother you with too many audit questions today." I made an effort not to run over to her every time I had a question. Instead, I worked through a series of tasks, compiled all the issues and then politely asked when would be a good time for us to sit and discuss. Would you believe that these simple acts went a long way, simple because I took the time to build a relationship. Eventually, the entire team started to strategize and would send me to the client with their queries because she was more responsive to me.

Don't Let Your Voice Go Silent

In most environments, there will always be that person who wants to stamp their authority as the boss even if they are not the boss. In those types of environments, opinions and ideas are shut down. The team is run on fear rather than respect. These are real life scenarios that I am bringing to you, that you are likely to have to navigate in your own career. People will dismiss your boundaries, push you into corners only if you allow them to. If I am to be honest, I allowed people to trample my boundaries. Some people say that with age comes wisdom, but I believe that it is experience that brings wisdom.

Always remember that you have a voice, and learning how to use that voice gives you power. Now I am not advocating for one to be rude, rough, and uncouth but stand firm on your principles. I once read a quote which said that "If you stand for nothing, you fall for everything." Here is a personal example. In the Caribbean, there is a religious group known as the Seventh Day Adventist. This group of Christians, set aside Saturday as their Sabbath and therefore do not work on Saturdays. This principle by which they operate is acknowledged and respected in the workplace. On the other hand, some employers do not show the same respect to Christians who worship on Sundays. In my early career I had to take a stance and express that my Sundays are for worship and that in the same manner that the employer would not ask a Seventh Day Adventist to abandon church on Saturday for the sake of work, I too should not be asked to abandon my church on Sundays. It was a bold move, but it was a necessary boundary that needed to be established so I stood firm on my principles. Do not let others dictate who you are. There will be times to give and times to take. There will be times of compromise and times of finding middle ground. There will be instances of differing views and opposing ideas. However, don't be afraid to share ideas, don't be afraid to make suggestions and don't be afraid to speak up.

Another dynamic that causes some struggles in the workplace is intergenerational issues. I recently attended a conference where the speaker delved into this topic in detail and for me, it made a lot of things make sense. The workplaces of today are now a mixture of persons from different generations, and each generation has a unique perspective of what the dynamics in the workplace should be. The older generations believe in hierarchy and that you must earn your place to contribute at the table. At the other extreme, the younger generations believe that their ideas and opinions matter too and a seat at the table is not defined by the number of years that you put into an organization but rather, by what you can contribute. Herein lies the clash of generations. This is one of those areas of finding middle ground. As I said earlier, you have a voice, but the key is in navigating how to let your voice be heard without offending the old stalwarts. If you have an idea or suggestion, the delivery of it is crucial. To take an approach of "nothing you guys are doing here makes sense" is a recipe for disaster. You cannot go into an organization and start pointing out everything that you think is wrong. People will become defensive, and your ideas and suggestions will not be heard or acknowledged because all that people will hear is criticism. Instead, a more tactful and softer approach can be taken. E.g. "I have observed the way this task is performed, but have you considered if we took this approach instead? Maybe this alternate method could save us some valuable time. Maybe we could look at the process a little closer together and see where there might be room for efficiency." The aim here is to create a space for collaboration rather than condemnation.

The last thing I want to leave with you in this chapter is:

Not Everyone Will See Your Worth, But It Is Important That You Do

The workplace is not set up to be a luxurious place. It boils down to the simple dynamic of you providing a service and receiving compensation for said service. Whilst it can be a place where friendships develop, it is also a place of rising tensions, undermining of character and sometimes even the breaking of spirits. One of the biggest lessons that I have learnt is do not be afraid to walk away. I remember distinctly working on an assignment with some new and unfamiliar concepts. It was not an area that I had any expertise in and neither did the leader of the assignment. The client themself was clueless. Yes, you read that right, the client was clueless. I had to reach out to our overseas office for guidance on the matter. I put in all the work. The leader of the assignment had very little involvement. He left me to handle it all on my own. During the assignment, he commended me for taking the lead, working with the overseas office, giving the client the guidance they needed and seeing the assignment through to the end. I felt good about that initial feedback, especially considering that this was my third assignment with this particular leader, and this was the first time that he acknowledged my existence. I felt a sense of pride knowing that I pulled it off. I persevered. It was a learning experience, and I handled it well. But as luck would have it, a few weeks later when providing me with the official feedback on the assignment, all the positive feedback he gave initially was replaced with nothing but negativity. It was as if a completely different individual was providing this feedback. I felt myself shrink smaller and smaller in the chair in his office as I fought hard to hold back my tears. That was the straw that broke the camel's back. That was a spirit breaking day. His words to me on that day initially was a blow to my self-confidence and my self-esteem. It was probably meant to crush me, but I eventually concluded that I was worth more than what he said I was. I concluded that I added value to the team and if he was not willing to acknowledge it, I would find a place that would. On that day I decided it was time to leave that organization because I did not feel valued there. I thought about it long and hard. I had no job offerings, no interviews lined up, but I knew that organization was no longer the place for me.

Whilst some of you reading this book may not be believers in God, I will still share this experience with you. I went home, drafted my resignation letter, signed, and dated it in advance for the end of the month, placed it in an envelope, took it to church, and placed it at the altar. That day I asked God for three things, the first of which was to provide me with a new job. In other words, I knew it was time to leave and I placed it in God's hands. The following week, I received a call unexpectedly, for a position that I had not submitted a résumé for. What started off as a chat about a potential role on a three-month contract, became the answer to a prayer. I make no exaggerations when I tell you that I was able to submit my resignation on the very exact day that I had dated it when I took it to church. I left my job of almost eleven years to take up a three-month contract. Some may call it a bold move; others may see it as a risky choice. Me, I call it faith. I understood my worth. That three-month contract was extended to six months, followed by a permanent position and two promotions in the next two years that followed. The corporate world can be cruel but sharpen your skills and seek to add value wherever you go. Some people will see your worth and some won't, but that is their loss. I left that job where I was made to feel inadequate and have continued to excel ever since leaving.

Doors have been opened even when I didn't go knocking, and I know that there are many more doors waiting to be opened. Having self-worth is key.

CHAPTER 8

EMBRACING LEADERSHIP OPPORTUNITIES

There are many people who long to be in leadership positions and others who run from or fear being leaders. There has been a long debate on whether leaders are born or developed. Some people naturally progress as leaders whilst others must unlearn old mindsets and learn new skills to fully be an effective leader. In accountancy, career development often leads to taking on leadership roles, but I dare say that everyone is not meant to be a leader and many times those who have strong desires to be leaders are often the most unfit for the job. This chapter is really geared towards those persons who may be fearful of stepping into leadership roles.

Allow me to speak from my personal experience here. Whilst I have held positions of leadership during my accounting career, in each instance I have been hesitant or fearful of the position. To be honest, I am quite comfortable with someone else making the decisions and giving the instructions whilst I execute. I am good at executing. Give me a task and a deadline and I am sure to deliver. However, the thought of being the decision maker often scared me and, in many instances, I felt that maybe I was not best suited for a leadership role. As life would have it, though not wanting to be in leadership positions, my life seemed to be set on that trajectory. I never pushed myself up for positions, I never sucked up with the hopes of it providing me with upward mobility, I just did my work honestly every day. Yet here I am speaking to you from a place of leadership.

When I speak about leadership, I am not speaking about being the head of a company, I am merely referring to abilities. The ability to see an issue and develop or suggest strategies to rectify it. The ability to motivate and encourage others. The ability to identify strengths in others and pull them out and help develop them. The ability to see weaknesses in people and instead of passing judgement, offer a hand to help close the gap. The ability to get others to buy into a vision and work as a cohesive team to achieve a goal. The ability to pay it forward, recognizing how people have invested in your career and taking the time to invest in someone else's career. The ability to share knowledge and pass on insight. In my mind, that is what makes an effective leader. I once heard a former boss of mine say that he will know that he has succeeded as an effective leader, once his department is able to fully function in his absence. It is about training up others to one day fill your position. Instilling confidence in others and helping them reach their full potential.

Leadership is all about trust. Someone may argue that it is about respect, but from my experience trust is the factor that really stands out. People must trust you to lead them. With leadership also comes a level of boldness. Sometimes, you may have to make the unpopular decision or take a stance and speak out whilst others choose to be silent. I am by no means attempting to make you run from a leadership position but rather helping you understand all the dynamics associated with it because as a leader the accountability falls on you.

Throughout my career I have fought with a concept known as Imposter Syndrome. What that meant is that I have often felt that I didn't belong in certain places. I felt like I was a fraud, pretending that I had it together and I knew it all, when deep inside, there was the feeling of falling short. I have doubted my own abilities and believed that my successes were by mere chance. When people attempted to congratulate me on my achievements, I downplayed them, brushing them off as being insignificant. I set high standards for myself not just in the work environment but also personally and would feel like a failure if I didn't hit the mark. If you have made it to this chapter, you will also realize that I spoke quite a bit about working hard. That in itself was an effect of the Imposter Syndrome, where I attempted to compensate for perceived weaknesses or inadequacies but overworking, fearful that people would see my weaknesses.

My most recent experience with Imposter Syndrome, relates to the current position I now hold as Assistant Vice President of Finance. I will confess that I was hesitant about applying for the role. The title itself scared me, although the role profile linked perfectly with the experience that I had acquired throughout my career. Others around me were encouraging me to "go for it" but I hesitated. I had numerous conversations with myself asking if I was good enough for this job, whether I would be able to get the work done. The day before the interview, I was a complete wreck, asking myself what I had gotten into. I felt overwhelmed and out of place. However, it helps to have a few people around who believe in you. They helped me to prepare and despite the nerves being high on the morning of the interview I felt a little more settled.

Fast forward a few months, I officially started the role but refused to update my social media pages to reflect such. I have seen many people update their LinkedIn Profile for much less and here I was with this grand promotion, and I was trying to keep it concealed. Why do you think that was so? First and foremost, I had a lot of "what ifs" going through my mind. What if I didn't meet the expectations of my new employer? What if I failed at the job in the first few months? What if I wouldn't be able to find another job after failing at this one? How ashamed I would be to have to retract any statements on social media about my promotion. It took me a while to settle into the role and with each day I asked myself the same questions repeatedly. Imposter Syndrome was strong and was leading me to believe that I was an imposter in this new role. The amazing thing is, that every time Imposter Syndrome raised its head in my life, there was always some external validation that eventually allowed me to believe that I earned my seat at the table, and I was right where I needed to be at that time.

Leadership is tricky, and it is amazing how I have evolved over the years. I now embrace leadership. Whilst I ran from it for several years, I have finally accepted that it flows naturally for me, and I am able to impact others positively. I wouldn't consider myself a complete overcomer from Imposter Syndrome, and the fear of leadership still lingers in the background sometimes. However, I have gotten better at managing those negative feelings by doing a few things.

- Acknowledging my achievements to date. A pat on the back isn't arrogance.
- Replacing negative feelings with positive affirmations. The words you speak over your life do matter.
- Be willing to accept failure. Many success stories often start with initial failure. The aim is to take the lesson from the failure and use it to propel you forward.
- Surrounding myself with a strong support system, whether it is a mentor, friend, or family member.
- Giving myself grace. This has been the hardest concept for me to apply. I am learning to be kind and compassionate to myself.

As you progress in your career, leadership opportunities will present themselves, some within the workplace and some may be external. Please don't allow your first response to be that of retreat. Some opportunities may be on the spot and with others you may have time to consider before deciding. In either case here are a few things that I want you to consider when placed in either situation.

Are You Qualified for The Task?

Consider the experiences that you have obtained to date. Do you have the know how to get it done? Has everything that you have learnt during your career led you to where you are now? A no answer to these questions does not automatically disqualify you from stepping into the role of leadership, but it is the starting point of assessing your suitability.

Would This Be a Good Learning Opportunity for You?

There are opportunities which will not bring with them a level of familiarity. It may be unknown territory. A path not trodden before. This may cause fear, fear of failure, fear of inadequacy. No one likes to walk into a situation that they don't have a proper handle of. Instead of thinking negatively, consider what you can take away from this experience if you succeed. Would this exposure further enhance your development?

Have You Bought into The Vision That You Are Being Asked to Lead?

You cannot be an effective leader if you have not embraced the vision. Some roles will call for you to be an agent of change. People will look to you as an example. What type of example will you be?

Your responses to the above can be a good gauge of whether you are ready to lead.

Some opportunities will come your way and in other instances, you may have to actively seek them out. If you don't consider yourself a natural leader, start small. Volunteer to take the lead on small projects whether in the workplace, professional organizations or even community initiatives. It could be something as simple as taking the lead on planning a games evening among friends. Harness your skills in spaces where you are allowed to fail gracefully. Seek feedback from the right people and apply the feedback to better yourself.

Don't count yourself out. You have what it takes!

CHAPTER 9

ACHIEVING WORK-LIFE INTEGRATION

Achieving work-life integration: what does that mean? Instead of integration, you have probably heard the term "Work Life Balance." What does this look like for a young aspiring accountant? I touched on this topic briefly in Chapter 4, but I will expand some more here.

Work-life integration is not specific to the field of accounting. Many professionals, young and old struggle with the concept of juggling work and life. Being good at what you do career wise often comes with a cost to your personal life, both physically and mentally. I know of persons who have taken a step down from their careers to be better able to manage their personal lives. The ultimate goal is to create or find a space where career progression and personal enjoyment or commitments can coexist.

Accounting is a fast-paced environment, driven by deadlines which might force us to push other elements of our lives aside at some point in time. The profession may cause us to believe that at month end, quarter end or year end, nothing should take precedence over our work. Sometimes we miss out on so many things in life for the sake of career progression. In the accountancy profession, without proper work life integration burnout becomes hard to avoid. There is no real reward for being the hardest working female or male if your mental health is being affected. What is the purpose of an astounding career, if you don't get to reap the rewards because your physical health is declining?

I have been labelled an overachiever by my siblings. In their words, anything that I set my mind to do, I must stand out at it. However, it has come with a steep price. I was always considered the sickly one in the family. To this day, there are still a number of ailments that I fight with constantly. On multiple occasions, I allowed work to be more important than my health. I worked long hours, ate poorly, and abandoned any form of physical activity. I suffer from migraines and recall one day the doctor was very concerned because a particular hormone level was so abnormal, she was fearful that I had a brain tumor. I did skull x-rays and some other tests, but luckily there was no abnormal growth on the brain. It was all attributable to the elevated level of stress that I was facing in the workplace. In another instance, because of poor eating choices when working late, skipping meals, and eating plenty of fast food, I was diagnosed as pre-diabetic. My doctor gave me a stern warning that If I didn't make specific changes in my life immediately that my quality of life would drastically decline. All these things occurred when I was still in my early twenties. Imagine that! At such an early age, working on my career and being plagued with sickness simply because I had not attempted to find work life balance.

I remember distinctly that completing my accounting designation was one of the hardest periods to navigate.

Working and studying was time consuming. Weekdays were long hours of work; weekends were either more long hours of work or classroom sessions. Once I completed my designation, I was confident that I would have more time to do the things I loved and the things that I kept putting off for a while. I was convinced that I would have lots of free time to hang out with friends and pick back up old hobbies. Sadly, that wasn't the case. The free time I anticipated was quickly filled with more work and those swimming lessons I promised to recommence went through the door along with several other things. Why am I telling you this? It is easy to get lost in your career. You may lose your purpose, your passion, or your sense of identity if you don't find a way to integrate work appropriately into your life.

It has taken me years to find some sense of balance, and even so, with every looming deadline or every new responsibility, it was as if I had to learn the concept of work life balance all over again. I don't wish to be one of those people who spend tireless hours committed to a job, waiting for retirement to really live and then never make it to retirement.

You are in charge of your own life. People can predict what they think you will become, but you alone determine who you will be.

Ever so often I must remind myself of the first line in the statement above. I am in charge of my own life. Church has always been present in my life, so I had to learn how to balance work, church, and my personal life, whilst maintaining my authentic self in the process. The way to take charge of your own life is to prioritize those things that mean the most to you. After vowing never to study again following the completion of my accounting designation, I felt compelled to do a course in Theology. Stage 1 was a one-year program followed by 2 more years, if willing to be more advanced. At the time, I didn't know how I was going to juggle it with work, but I knew that I wanted to do it and do it well. The first step was indicating to my superiors that on two evenings each week I would be unavailable to work late. I had to build up the courage to have that conversation and then be disciplined enough to pull myself away from work promptly at 4:30pm. Taking that step did me good. I completed the full three years and earned the title of valedictorian in both Year 1 and Year 3. In this instance, I set clear boundaries by defining what my work hours would be on the days on which I had classes. I communicated those boundaries and then I stuck to the schedule.

Do you know what I also learned in this work life integration journey?

- *Not everyone needs to know the things that you are doing in your spare time.*

The reason I say this is because people will attempt to define the value of what you do in your spare time. Whilst it may be important to you, they may view it as insignificant and therefore attempt to dissuade you from doing it or convince you that work is more important. Remember, you decide what is of value to you.

Another essential element of work life integration is to explore what self-care looks like for you. Many of us talk about self-care but how it is envisioned or defined differs from person to person. A leisurely stroll along the beach in the evening may work for one person. A nice massage every month may tick the box for someone else. Heading to the movies might be the preferred go to by one person whereas for another they may just want to go home and have some quiet time or snuggle up with a book. Whatever your preference, make a list of your self-care needs. You might be surprised that you have multiple options. Indicate the frequency by which you would like to do these things. Schedule them in your calendar accordingly and stick to it as much as possible. Bear in mind that as you grow, different things may become a priority for self-care, so be sure to revise the list as needed. Give your job a good effort but apply a greater effort for yourself.

There are a number of simple techniques which can also aid in work life balance. E.g. developing a schedule, whether daily or weekly, you decide. The purpose of the schedule is to ensure that you manage your day according to your commitments. The intention here is to establish a routine, carving out time for work, family, friends, and other personal activities. Pencil important items into your calendar with reminders. Block out specific times in your day for lunch. Skipping lunch has been a unique feature of accountants for way too long. Create a to do list for work but ensure that your list for the day is realistic i.e. can it be accomplished all in one day? Avoid cramming too many items into your schedule. The schedule must be practical. Scheduling too many items to accomplish within one day will either leave you feeling overwhelmed, frustrated, or burnt out.

- *It is okay to say no.*

Sometimes we put undue pressure on ourselves by taking on more than we should. Contrary to popular belief, not every task is urgent. No one will die. I repeat, no one will die. There are some ask that can be politely declined by indicating that you simply don't have the capacity to take on anything more at this time. It is okay to decline tasks, but the communication of the "no" must be professional and tactful. Prioritization of tasks is key. You do not need to take on everything at the same time or by yourself. Everything isn't urgent and if you do it all yourself, you rob others of the ability to grow and develop.

We live in the social media age, and very often work creeps into our personal time, because we allow our personal time to creep into work time. Let's be honest with ourselves, how many times a day do you sit idly by during work hours scrolling through social media, or chatting away with friends? We have a task that needs to be done, but we don't want to do it, so we procrastinate, taking in everything social media has to offer. Fast forward a few days, the deadline is around the corner, and you are now struggling to complete the task. You are upset because you have to work late, but really whose fault is it? What I am trying to say is that sometimes to find that perfect integration, we have to limit some of the distractions around us. During your working hours create an environment which allows you to be focused on work with minimal distractions.

The last tip I want to leave with you in this chapter is:

- ***Don't be afraid to move on if your current space does not meet your needs.***

Many of us get comfortable in our jobs even when they are draining us. There is typically a fear of trying something new or navigating an unfamiliar environment. Not every organization will have a culture of work life balance, and not every employer will care about your personal needs. The onus is therefore on you to find an environment that is the right fit for you; an environment where there is room for growth and development, whilst giving you space to live at the same time. Create the life you want because you only have one shot at it.

CHAPTER 10

LOOKING TO THE FUTURE

The starting point of your individual careers will vary from person to person; however, each has the potential to be shaped into something phenomenal. Where you start sets the foundation and significantly influences your career success. Fundamentals which need to be embedded from the very start, despite where you start include having the foundation skills, developing good work ethics and habits, especially being disciplined, and building a solid reputation. The path you take will not be the same, but a destination of success is attainable, if you carefully navigate the road before you, knowing when to pause, slow down or take a different path.

Looking to the future is linked in many ways to your past. People often say that your past doesn't define you. I have had that line drilled into my head on countless occasions. Today however, I chose to phrase it differently. How you view your past defines your future. In life there are always mistakes that will be made, lessons to be learned, losses to be had, disappointments to be experienced. However, it is our perception and reaction toward these things that impact our future the most. The experiences of our past quite often shape our behavior and contribute in some way to the future. An initial setback in life doesn't make you a failure and failure doesn't mean you will never succeed. A late start in your career doesn't disqualify you from success. Analyze the past, take what you can from it and apply those takeaways towards securing a successful future. Someone once said that in order to move forward we must acknowledge the past. Setbacks in the past teach us what not to repeat again. Wins in the past teach us the correct formula to apply to keep winning. Looking to the future whilst acknowledging your past will give you a good vision for the future.

The accounting journey has many potholes, speed bumps and even some dead ends. Yet there is a future of success that awaits you if you keep pressing on. This is why having long-term goals is important. It gives you a goal post to aim towards, something to focus on. The mindset that you have now will determine how far you propel into the future. If you think you can, you will. If you think you will fail, you likely will. A go-getter attitude is what you need. If your approach is that life will miraculously grant you all your desires with little effort required on your part, you won't get very far. However, if you earnestly work towards the things you desire, you are most certainly on your way to success. You must see yourself where you want to be in a few years and start modelling the future you want from now.

Dress For Success

I always knew I wanted to be successful. Some people may look at me now, at the way I dress and carry myself and think that I always had it altogether. However, I remember starting my first job with six suits of clothes. This meant that I wore the same outfits every week with the exception of one day when I would interchange outfit number six. I didn't come from a well-off family and my parents did their best to give my siblings and I just what we needed. Every weekend I had to wash those suits to be able to have clean clothes for the following week. Was that something that I was ashamed of; no. I wore my clothes with pride and ensured that I looked professional every day. I ensured that the way I carried myself was a positive reflection of my employers and aligned to my work ethic. Even at that early stage my attire, my character, my approach to work were always a product of my desire to succeed.

Be Confident in Who You Are

If I had to walk into a professional space now, people might think "well there goes a confident young lady." What people don't know or see are the many challenges I faced as I navigated this space over the years. Every hurdle, each obstacle, all the setbacks, had a lesson in it for me. Each moment of frustration was a character-building moment. I remember being completely fed up with one job, and I would say frequently "Whatever lesson this environment is supposed to teach me, let it teach me quickly because I am ready to go". I have met people who were difficult to work with, but it helped me to refine my softer skills. I have been overlooked at times, but it taught me patience and that timing is everything. I have learnt that it is not perfection that we should strive for, but rather continuous improvement. I have learnt to be resilient and most importantly I have been able to see what I bring to the table. I no longer shy away from offering an opinion on a matter or suggesting how things can be improved. Where I once felt intimidated and uncertain, I am now confident that I do good work and have developed the boldness to speak about things which don't sit well with me. Most importantly I have learnt to walk away from environments which add no value to my life whether professionally or personally.

Wherever you are in your career right now, whether at the very beginning or somewhere in the middle feeling stuck, be reassured that there is room for you at the table once you are intentional about succeeding. The future is now. The work that you put in now paves the way for the future you desire. The way you respond to setbacks now, forms the pillars and building blocks for the future. Stay resilient, adaptable, curious, and proactive and the future will become clearer. Ask yourself these questions: what is my vision for the future? What are my ambitions? What do I wish to achieve in this lifetime? The best way to get to where you are going is to know where you are going in the first place. Without a destination, you will ramble a lot. Set out the road map. The future is yours to seize.

Stay Up to Date with Emerging Trends

From a more technical standpoint, technology is advancing in a way that we have never imagined before. Whether we wish to accept it or not, Artificial Intelligence (AI) is now being embedded in everything we do. Looking towards the future as an accountant means being aware of emerging trends and equipping yourself to stay up to date with such trends. Be open minded about how AI can be used in the accounting space and look for opportunities to train or learn to use AI. Artificial Intelligence is able to transform the role of the accountant. The typical accountant now still relies heavily on spreadsheets for reporting and day-to-day activities. Whilst many are afraid that AI will take over their jobs, the accountant is uniquely positioned for AI to take over the mundane routine tasks. Instead of hours spent creating files, the click of a button will soon give us dashboards of valuable information. Such strides in technology will allow the accountant to be more forward-thinking and proactive, supporting businesses in their needs for growth and development. The key is to be agile if you are to remain relevant.

My vision for the future is to see more people who look like me, black females, find a place and their voice in a field that is mostly male dominated. In many spaces across the world, there are unique challenges with being a female and secondly being black. For centuries black people didn't have a voice and for women, their opinions were not valued. The world we live in now however, has levelled the playing field to some extent and women, more importantly black women now have access to the same education that their counterparts were privy to before. However, education opens the door but does not necessarily get you through it. Some women are yet to genuinely believe in themselves and understand that their voice matters. My aim is to help women be bold enough to step through the door that has been opened. I wish to see young women sitting around Board tables making valuable contributions to the prospects of their various organizations. For too long, women have had to take a back seat in the corporate world. Men held positions of CEOs and CFOs. Whilst women are present in Finance environments, the "elite" roles are held by men with women being seen as providing a supporting function. It is time for the tide to change. It is time for women to step out from the shadows and make their mark in Board rooms across the globe. I was completely blown away when I saw the CFO of my current organization walk into a Board Meeting in a pink pants suit. Little did she know that for me that was such an empowering statement. To me it said, "I earned my spot here and so I am free to express myself here." The future is as bright as you make it and luckily, there are some forerunners ahead of you, who are already shaking up the ground. The footpath has been started, now it is time for you to add your own stone.

CHAPTER 11

ACHIEVING SUCCESS

The definition of success varies from person to person and even more importantly, it varies depending on the stage you are at in life. For a university leaver, success may look like obtaining a job within a well-known organization. For someone already in the workforce, a promotion, or the opportunity to lead and effectively execute a project may tick the box for success. The amazing thing about success is that it isn't fixed. It is a moving goal post, and you alone get to define what reflects success for you at any given point in time. Success is ever evolving. What may symbolize achievement today might change as you grow and your aspirations shift. Success comes in various forms, professional milestones, personal achievements, or impacting the lives of others positively. The key is to understand that attaining success is about the journey and not solely about the destination. It is about learning and growing through each experience, ensuring that you align your achievements with your values and dreams.

To ensure that you are constantly on a path to success, you must acknowledge your growth, recognizing that each challenge overcome, each goal attained is a stepping stone bringing you closer to a place of self-fulfillment. Each one is a reminder of your resilience and determination. Keep moving your goal post, keep striving for more, and most importantly, keep defining success on your own terms.

There are a few distinct moments in my life which at the time I considered milestones in my journey to success. The biggest accomplishment for me was completing my accounting designation. It was demanding work, but I stayed the course. I was overjoyed to be able to tick that one off my list. Another milestone was being promoted to manager in one of the Big Four Audit Firms. If you are familiar with these companies, you know that they hire the best of the best, so there is tight competition to be selected for the few available spots of manager. To be honest, it was at this level that I felt like I had finally made it. I saw this milestone as confirmation that I was good enough to tackle whatever challenge was thrown my way. Promotion to this level was a testimony of not just hard work but confirmation that I had both the technical skills to get the work done and the softer skills required to effectively lead a team. It was symbolic of attaining the right balance in my career development. Beyond reaching the level of manager, I had no immediate goals in sight. At that time, this was success, and I was okay there. A few years in however, I felt the need to move and progress. What I wanted to do next, I was not sure of, but I knew that I had outgrown my current environment. Success was also having the opportunity to mentor three young ladies, two of which I have maintained contact with, and I am immensely proud of their professional progress. I was their advocate, their listening ear, and their motivator.

I have since transitioned to the industry and made strides in other fields. For me, whilst I am happy with my career progression, I do not believe that my journey to success is completed. True success will come when I can usher young aspiring accountants into a safe working environment. A space where their growth and development are catered to, a space where their opinions matter, a space where they can contribute freely, and collaboration is encouraged. Success for me, will be attained at the point when my life story can impact lives and motivate others to tap into their greatest self and truest potential. My passion is to pay it forward, to mentor those who might have started just where I did, as a timid university student. My goal is to instill values such as an excellent work ethic, accountability, and dependability. To help those who unfortunately might battle with the anxieties associated with the profession and foster belief in self. To help young persons to be able to express themselves freely but professionally and harness the technical skills required to guarantee that the future of accountancy is in good hands.

My next measure of success is to publish more books like this one, simply to help people navigate life by sharing my life experiences.

As you chart your own path for success, remember these five things:

- You define your success. You are the captain of your ship. Set your goals and steer your ship towards them.
- It is okay to change paths or pivot along the way. One's vision today, might not be one's vision tomorrow. Life happens, priorities change. It doesn't mean that you have failed, you simply need to pivot.

- Be your biggest cheerleader. Not everyone will cheer you on along this journey. Some people will sit grudgeful because of your victories and wait for you to fail. The onus is on you to celebrate your wins whether big or small.
- Believe in yourself. If you think you can't, you won't. Everything seems impossible until it gets done.
- Delayed does not always mean denied. Close doors or what might be perceived as missed opportunities may be aligning you for something greater.

Success is yours to attain. If you want it, go get it.

CHAPTER 12

CONCLUSION

As I reflect on my journey, from the early days of uncertainty to the moments of triumph, I am reminded that every challenge faced, and every milestone achieved has shaped who I am today. My path in the world of accounting has been one of growth, perseverance, and relentless pursuit of excellence.

Your journey to success will look completely different from mine. My encouragement to you is to set clear goals and work diligently towards them. Never underestimate the power of hard work and dedication. Be ethical and professional in all your dealings, hold fast to your values and let integrity guide your decisions.

Understand that setbacks and challenges will present themselves but be mindful of your response. Seize every opportunity that gives you exposure and experience to ultimately aid in your growth and development. Success is often a path trodden alone for many, but it does not have to be that way for you. Associate with like-minded people, seek out mentors who inspire and challenge you and surround yourself with those who lift you up.

Lastly, I implore you to pay it forward. The accounting profession is not just about numbers and balance sheets;

it is about making a difference, creating value, and driving positive change in the world. Let it be your desire to help someone along the way, in whatever way. Be an example and a beacon of support for others on their paths. Don't be afraid to open doors for others to walk through. The guidance that I have given to you, I wished that I had it at inception. Unfortunately, I had to figure some things out along the way. You too will have a few things that you will have to learn on your own, but I trust that this book will help you navigate your journey a little better. My journey is far from over, but I am doing my part to ensure that the future of the accountancy profession is in good hands.

The future is full of possibilities, and your dreams are within reach. Continue to learn, grow, and break through barriers knowing that your contributions matter. Your success is not just measured by the titles you hold or the accolades you receive, but by the impact you make and the legacy you leave.

In closing, I urge you to stay curious, remain resilient, and always strive for balance. As you move forward, may you find fulfillment in your work and joy in your achievements. Your journey is just beginning, and the best is yet to come.

Here's to your future, to your breakthroughs, and to the endless possibilities that lie ahead.

"Very relatable. Impressed with the author's honesty and transparency. A recommended read for the young aspiring accountant."

Lisa Moore, HR Director

"This personal account of Shakira's journey to enter and progress within the accounting profession provides meaningful insights for those considering this career path. While our journeys are unique, Shakira has provided a very candid perspective on the challenges she faced in her journey, some of which may also be encountered by others entering the profession. Beyond accountancy, I believe this story will resonate with those pursuing other professional careers as well. I am incredibly proud of Shakira for sharing her story with a view to encourage the next generation of leaders."

Kathryn Jenkins, Chief Financial Officer

"In her book Balance Sheets and Breakthroughs, Shakira Johnson takes readers on her accounting journey from a young university graduate to her Finance Vice Presidency role. She shares insights that are beneficial to individuals across all professions. Not only does she provide strategies for addressing various challenges in the workplace and on the professional journey, but she provides solid strategies for leadership growth and development. The incorporation of her personal experiences with practical lessons creates a connection with readers. Balance Sheets & Breakthroughs offers reality-based strategies and insights to those who want more, who want to stand out, advance and make a difference personally and professionally. This is a must read!!"

Major Merna Riley-desVignes, SHRM-SCP, MSc (HRD), BScN, CNA, RM, RN, John Maxwell Certified Coach, Trainer, Teacher and Speaker, Consultant (Leadership, Management, Healthcare and Industrial Relations)

Made in the USA
Columbia, SC
07 January 2025